LUCY ISAACS

END ANXIETY

The Essential Guide on How to Overcome Anxiety
and Live Stress Free, Discover The Proven Methods
on How to Reduce the Stress in Your Life

Descrierea CIP a Bibliotecii Naționale a României
LUCY ISAACS
    END ANXIETY. The Essential Guide on How to Overcome
Anxiety and Live Stress Free, Discover The Proven Methods on
How to Reduce the Stress in Your Life / Lucy Isaacs – Bucharest:
Editura My Ebook, 2021
    ISBN

LUCY ISAACS

END ANXIETY

The Essential Guide on How to Overcome Anxiety and Live Stress Free, Discover The Proven Methods on How to Reduce the Stress in Your Life

My Ebook Publishing House
Bucharest, 2021

TABLE OF CONTENTS

INTRODUCTION

These days everyone is feeling pressure. We rush at work, we rush at home, there's always so much that needs to be done. Stress and anxiety have become part of our lives. But how do we deal with it? Most people don't. Stress causes havoc on our bodies. Let it rage free and stress will make you sick.

The statistics are staggering. One in every eight Americans between the age of 18 and 54 suffers from an anxiety disorder. This totals over 19 million people! Research conducted by the National Institute of Mental Health has shown that anxiety disorders are the most common mental illness, surpassing even depression. Women are affected almost twice as much as men and it's the number one mental health problem among this gender. Men are not unaffected though; anxiety disorders in males are second only to alcohol and drug abuse.

Anxiety not on takes a toll on our health but on our checkbooks, to the tune of $46.6 billion annually in the United

States. Anxiety sufferers see an average of five doctors before being successfully diagnosed.

Stress and anxiety go hand in hand. One of the major symptoms of stress is anxiety. And stress accounts for 80 percent of all illnesses either directly or indirectly.

Stress is more dangerous than originally thought. You probably already know that it can raise your blood pressure, increasing the likelihood of a stroke. But recently it's been claimed that 90 percent of visits to a primary care physician were because of stress-related disorders.

Health Psychology magazine reports that chronic stress can interfere with the normal function of the body's immune system. And studies have proven that stressed individuals have an increased vulnerability to catching an illness and are more susceptible to allergic, autoimmune, or cardiovascular diseases. Doctors agree that during chronic stress, the functions of the body that are nonessential to survival, such as the digestive and immune systems, shut down. Stress is making us sick.

Furthermore, stress often prompts people to respond in unhealthy ways such as smoking, drinking alcohol, eating poorly, or becoming physically inactive. This damages the body in addition to the wear and tear of the stress itself.

You can't eliminate stress; it's part of life. You can however manage it. It's how we react to it that makes the difference. Coping techniques will help you control stress so that you can maintain your health and happiness.

I have suffered from anxiety disorders caused by stress for years. I've learned ways to cope and some dealing mechanisms that help me manage it. This book is a combination of my own experiences and advice from experts. It will provide you with tools that that you can use when your in a stressful situation.

I've also outlined different ways that you can face debilitating anxiety and panic attacks. Plus I will share some amazing information that has helped me. Let's reduce the effects of stress and anxiety from your life!

WHY ARE WE SO STRESSED OUT?

We're living in very trying and difficult times. Technology and advancements have made things more complicated than the simple life our ancestors had. Sometimes life can be terribly painful and unfair. Why do some people manage to get through it easier than others? They have better tools.

Society as a whole is more stressed. Millions of people are in record levels of debt. Many are losing their jobs, their homes, their health and sometimes even their sanity. Worry, depression and anxiety seem to have become a way of life.

It seems like we've entered the Age of Anxiety. In fact, Time magazine once proclaimed this in one of their issues. The constant stress and uncertainties of living in the 21st century have certainly taken their toll. The result is that many people are now living in a state of constant fear and worry.

When the 9/11 terrorist attacks happened, this became magnified. In fact, even now, years later, people report they are still scared everyday. They worry that something of that magnitude will happen again.

Turn on the news or open up a newspaper and you're bombarded with disturbing images and stories. You begin to wonder if you're safe anywhere. The information age is providing us access to endless data. Most of what is covered by the media is unsettling and disturbing news.

Having more women in the workplace adds to the stress. Many women feel the need to be everything to everyone and that includes a paycheck earner, housekeeper, mother, wife, daughter, and sibling. Trying to cram everything in and do it well is a huge stress factor. Women are so busy doing, that they don't make for themselves and if they do they feel guilt. This cycle is a losing one and it's driving stress levels to an all-time high.

Even children can feel the pressure of stress and anxiety. Teenagers who want to go to college feel pressure to obtain scholarships. They need part-time jobs to earn money for extras that their parents can no longer afford. Add peer pressure into the mix and you have a veritable pressure cooker!

Cell phones, Internet, palm pilots, blackberries, I-pods – we are always on the go and always reachable. There's no downtime in life any more. We're so busy that we've forgotten how to relax and our minds are constantly going over what needs to be done.

We feel pressure to do these things because we think we HAVE to, not because we WANT to. It's difficult for people to just say "No". Not saying that one little word piles up un-needed expectations and obligations that make us feel anxious.

All of us will experience situations that may cause us to become stressed or feel anxious. The reasons are endless but here's a few common stress triggers; buying a property, career pressures, having guests stay over, being bullied, exams, looking after children, managing finances, relationship issues, deaths, illnesses and even traveling. Stress is a 'normal' function of everyday life. Only when it starts to take over you life does it become a problem.

Everyone reacts to stressful situations differently. It's usually when we don't feel in control of a situation, that we feel its grip tightening around us causing extreme stress. Regain that control and lose the stress.

You have everything inside you that you need to overcome stress and the accompanying anxiety. You can gain the upper hand on stress.

Let's first look at the barriers we put up that are preventing us from becoming healthy and getting rid of our anxiety and stress.

BLOCKING BEHAVIORS KEEPING
YOUR STRESS ALIVE

There are three obsessive behaviors that you are likely to be engaging in that impeded your healing process and stop you from enjoying life. Recognizing these barriers is the first step toward getting rid of the problems that happen when you're too stressed.

The first is obsessive negativity. When you are obsessively negative, it means that you have a tendency toward looking at all the things you don't like about people, places, situations, and things in your life. Is your cup half full or half empty? I believe it's half full and you can too.

If your internal voice is telling you things like, "You can't do this!" or "No one understands!" or "Nothing ever works", you're sending yourself negative signals. You may be doing this unconsciously so you need to tune into this voice. It could be holding you back from knowing what it's like to view life from a

14

positive lens and enjoy the beauty in yourself and people around you! There's a whole world out there for you...with happiness and positive thinking.

Then you have obsessive perfectionism. When you engage in obsessive perfectionism, you are centered on trying to do everything "just so" to the point of driving yourself into an anxious state of being. You may find yourself making statements such as, "I have to do this right, or I'll be a failure!" or "If I am not precise, people will be mad at me or won't like me!" Again, this behavior may be totally under the threshold of your awareness, but it interferes greatly with your ability to enjoy things without feeling "uptight" and "stressed."

Finally there is obsessive analysis. When you are obsessed about analyzing things, you find yourself wanting to re-hash a task or an issue over and over again. For instance, you might find yourself making statements such as, "I need to look this over, study it, and know it inside and out...or else I can't relax!" or "If I relax and let things go without looking them over repeatedly, things go wrong!"

While analytical thinking is an excellent trait, if it's done in excess you never get to stop and smell the roses because you're too busy trying to analyze everything and everyone around you. Gaining insight into this type of behavior is one of the most important keys to letting go of stress, and getting complete power over your anxiety.

If you find yourself engaging in any of the above "Blocking Behaviors", there are two things you can do to help yourself. First, ask the people you know, love, and trust, "Am I negative about things?" "Do I complain a lot?" and "Am I difficult to be around?" This may be hard for you to listen to, as the truth sometimes hurts. But the insight you will get from others' assessment of you is invaluable. You'll know precisely how others see you. Accept their comments as helpful information, and you'll gain insight about yourself.

Second, keep a journal to write down and establish patterns of when you are using "blocking behaviors." Even if you are not thrilled with the idea of writing, you can make little entries into a notebook or journal each day. The great part is that you'll begin to see patterns in your behavior that reveal exactly what you're doing to prevent yourself from curing your anxiety.

We'll give you some great stress busting techniques later in the book, but you need to recognize these blockages first so you can move into the "healing" stage and conquer your stress and anxiety.

Many people think that stress and anxiety is the same thing. This couldn't be further from the truth!

STRESS OR ANXIETY

Contrary to popular belief, there is a difference between stress and anxiety. Stress comes from the pressures we feel in life, as we are pushed by work or any other task that puts undue pressure on our minds and body, adrenaline is released, extended stay of the hormone causes depression, a rise in the blood pressure and other negative changes and effects.

One of these negative effects is anxiety. With anxiety, fear overcomes all emotions accompanied by worry and apprehension, making a person a recluse and full of jitters. Other symptoms are chest pains, dizziness, and shortness of breath and panic attacks.

Stress is caused by an something happening in your life now. Anxiety is stress that continues after that stressor is gone. Stress can come from any situation or thought that makes you feel frustrated, angry, nervous, or even anxious. What is stressful to one person is not necessarily stressful to another.

Anxiety is a feeling of apprehension or fear and is almost always accompanied by feelings of impending doom. The source of this uneasiness is not always known or recognized, which can add to the distress you feel.

Stress is the way our bodies and minds react to something which upsets our normal balance in life. An example of stress is the response we feel when we are frightened or threatened. During stressful events our adrenal glands release adrenaline, a hormone, which activates our body's defense mechanisms causing our hearts to pound, blood pressure to rise, muscles to tense, and the pupils of our eyes to dilate.

A principal indication of increased stress is an escalation in your pulse rate; however, a normal pulse rate doesn't necessarily mean you aren't stressed. Constant aches and pains, palpitations, anxiety, chronic fatigue, crying, over or under- eating, frequent infections, and a decrease in your sexual desire are signs that indicate that you might be under stress.

Of course, every time we are under stress, we do not react to such an extreme and we are not always under such great duress or fear every time we are confronted with a stressful situation.

Some people are more susceptible than others to stress. For some, even ordinary daily decisions seem insurmountable.
18

Deciding what to have for dinner or what to buy at the store, is a seemingly, monumental dilemma for them. On the other hand, there are those people, who seem to thrive under stress by becoming highly productive being driven by the force of pressure.

Research shows women who have children have higher levels of stress related hormones in their blood than women without children. Does this mean women without children don't experience stress? Absolutely not!

It means that women without children may not experience stress as often or to the same degree which women with children do. This means for women with children, it's particularly important to schedule time for yourself; you will be in a better frame of mind to help your children and meet the daily challenge of being a parent, once your stress level is reduced.

Anxiety, on the other hand, is a feeling of unease. Everybody experiences it when faced with a stressful situation, for example before an exam or an interview, or during a worrying time such as illness. It is normal to feel anxious when facing something difficult or dangerous and mild anxiety can be a positive and useful experience.

However, for many people, anxiety interferes with normal life. Excessive anxiety is often associated with other psychiatric conditions, such as depression. Anxiety is considered abnormal when it is very prolonged or severe, it happens in the absence of a stressful event, or it is interfering with everyday activities such as going to work.

The physical symptoms of anxiety are caused by the brain sending messages to parts of the body to prepare for the "fight or flight" response. The heart, lungs and other parts of the body work faster. The brain also releases stress hormones, including adrenaline. Common indicators of excessive anxiety include:

- Diarrhea
- Dry mouth
- Rapid heartbeat or palpitations
- Insomnia
- Irritability or anger
- Inability to concentrate
- Fear of being "crazy"
- Feeling unreal and not in control of your actions which is called depersonalization

Anxiety can be brought on in many ways. Obviously, the presence of stress in your life can make you have anxious thoughts. Many people who suffer from anxiety disorders occupy their minds with excessive worry. This can be worry about anything from health matters to job problems to world issues.

Certain drugs, both recreational and medicinal, can also lead to symptoms of anxiety due to either side effects or withdrawal from the drug. Such drugs include caffeine, alcohol, nicotine, cold remedies, and decongestants, bronchodilators for asthma, tricyclic antidepressants, cocaine, amphetamines, diet pills, ADHD medications, and thyroid medications.

A poor diet can also contribute to stress or anxiety -- for example, low levels of vitamin B12. Performance anxiety is related to specific situations, like taking a test or making a presentation in public. Post-traumatic stress disorder (PTSD) is a stress disorder that develops after a traumatic event like war, physical or sexual assault, or a natural disaster.

In very rare cases, a tumor of the adrenal gland (pheochromocytoma) may be the cause of anxiety. This happens because of an overproduction of hormones responsible for the feelings and symptoms of anxiety.

While anxiety may seem a bit scary, what's even scarier is that excessive anxiety and stress can lead to depression. Suffering from depression can be a lifelong struggle, but the good news is that all of this is manageable!

So, let's take a few little quizzes to see if you are suffering from too much stress, excessive anxiety, or depression.

QUIZ TIME!

Before you begin here, you need to know that we are not medical professionals. This information has come from reliable sources and isn't meant to be a complete diagnostic tool in any way. These quizzes are simply guidelines to help you recognize any problems you might have and be able to effectively deal with those problems.

Because depression can be the most serious of our topics, let's start by seeing if you may be depressed. Keep in mind that everyone has his or her "blue" days. The thing that separates clinical depression from simple melancholy is that the symptoms occur over a period of time. They don't come and go, they stay around for a while and can affect your life adversely.

Ask yourself the following questions. Answer yes if you've been feeling this way consistently over a period of two weeks.

1. Do you find yourself constantly sad?

2. Are you un-motivated to do simple things like shower, clean up the house, or make dinner?

3. Do people tell you you're overly irritable?

4. Do you have trouble concentrating?

5. Are you feeling isolated from family and friends even when they are around you?

6. Have you lost interest in your favorite activities?

7. Do you feel hopeless, worthless, or guilty for no reason at all?

8. Are you always tired and have trouble sleeping?

9. Has your weight fluctuated significantly?

If you can answer, "Yes" to five or more of these questions, you could be suffering from clinical depression. It is important for you to seek out the help of a medical professional whether that is a doctor or a therapist. There are many medications out there that can help with depression.

I always tried to deny my own depression, but once I began taking an anti-depressant, I couldn't believe what a difference that one pill a day made! It gave me freedom from the "black hole" I had fallen into and helped me enjoy life again. If you think you are depressed, ACT NOW! You deserve to be happy!

Let's see if stress and anxiety are taking over in your life. Ask yourself the following:

1. Do you worry constantly and talk to yourself negatively?

2. Do you have difficulty concentrating?

3. Do you get mad and react easily?

4. Do you have recurring neck or headaches?

5. Do you grind your teeth?

6. Do you frequently feel overwhelmed, anxious or depressed?

7. Do you feed your stress with unhealthy habits such as eating or drinking excessively, smoking, arguing, or avoiding yourself and life in other ways?

8. Do small pleasures fail to satisfy you?

9. Do you experience flashes of anger over a minor problem?

If you can answer "Yes" to most of these questions, then you do have excessive stress in your life. The good news is that you've bought this book and you'll learn many valuable techniques to cope with that stress. But we'll get to that later!

Let's move on to anxiety.

1. Do you experience shortness of breath, heart palpitation or shaking while at rest?

2. Do you have a fear of losing control or going crazy?

3. Do you avoid social situations because of fear?

4. Do you have fears of specific objects?

5. Do you fear that you will be in a place or situation from which you cannot escape?

6. Do you feel afraid of leaving your home?

7. Do you have recurrent thoughts or images that refuse to go away?

8. Do you feel compelled to perform certain activities repeatedly?

9. Do you persistently relive an upsetting event from the past?

Answering "Yes" to more than four of these questions can indicate an anxiety disorder.

Suffering from depression, too much stress, or excessive anxiety can endanger your overall health and it's time to take steps to overcome this – RIGHT NOW!

Stress and anxiety affects many factors in our body not only in our mental state. Cancer and other deadly diseases are related to stress and anxiety because of the changes in the chemical composition in our body.

Don't be a victim of stress and anxiety. Discipline, a proper schedule and knowing your limitations will help. Learn your limitations and stick to it. Do not over exert yourself. Just try to go over the border an inch at a time.

You can lead a productive successful and fulfilling life and career without endangering your health. Living with anxiety will slowly kill you while driving your family and friends away.

Stress and anxiety can lead to panic attacks, which can be a serious situation. Let's explore that subject a little more.

PANIC ATTACKS

One of the unfortunate outcomes from suffering from excessive stress and anxiety is a physical reaction of your body to the situation. It's like your body is telling you that you need to rest for a moment. Except when you're having a panic attack, it's anything BUT restful.

I had my first panic attack while my husband and I were driving home from a football game. We were about 30 miles from our home when I began to feel a bit "off". I was having trouble breathing, my body felt disconnected, and my heart was beating at what seemed like 90 miles an hour.

I pulled the van off to the side of the highway and got out hoping to "walk it off". But that didn't work. No matter what I tried, I couldn't catch my breath. I felt like I was dying. I remember saying over and over again, "Please not now. I'm not ready." It was horrifying.

The good news; I wasn't dying. But that night was the beginning of a terrible journey for me. Stress had taken over my life and was now effecting my entire body. Since then, I have had many panic attacks and I've learned how to recognize that one is coming and how to control it.

Let's look at the signs of and impending panic attack.

- Palpitations
- A pounding heart, or an accelerated heart rate
- Sweating
- Trembling or shaking
- Shortness of breath
- A choking sensation
- Chest pain or discomfort
- Nausea or stomach cramps
- De-realization (a feeling of unreality)
- Fear of losing control or going crazy
- Fear of dying
- Numbness or a tingling sensation in your face and limbs
- Chills or hot flashes

You would be surprised at how many people go to the hospital emergency room completely sure that they're having a heart attack only to find out that it's a panic attack. They're that intense!

It's very difficult for your loved ones to imagine or even understand what you are going through when you have a panic attack. They may lose patience with you, tell you to "get over it", or think you're faking. It may help if you show them the following scenario.

You are standing in line at the grocery store. It's been a long wait but there's only one customer to go before you make it to the cashier. Wait, what was that?

An unpleasant feeling forms in your throat, your chest feels tighter, now a sudden shortness of breath, and what do you know - your heart skips a beat. "Please, God, not here."

You make a quick scan of the territory - is it threatening? Four unfriendly faces are behind you and one person is in front. Pins and needles seem to prick you through your left arm, you feel slightly dizzy, and then the explosion of fear as you dread the worst. You are about to have a panic attack.

There is no doubt in your mind that this is going to be a big one. Okay, time for you to focus. You know how to deal with this – at least you hope you do! Start breathing deeply - in through the nose, out through the mouth.

Think relaxing thoughts, and again, while breathing in, think "Relax," and then breathe out. But it doesn't seem to be having any positive effect; in fact, just concentrating on breathing is making you feel self-conscious and more uptight.

Maybe if you just try to relax your muscles. Tense both shoulders, hold for 10 seconds, then release. Try it again. Nope, still no difference. The anxiety is getting worse and the very fact that you are out of coping techniques worsens your panic. If only you were with a family member or close friend, then you could feel more confident in dealing with this situation.

The adrenaline is pumping through your system; your body is tingling with uncomfortable sensations. You feel like you are losing complete control of your emotions. No one around you has any idea of the sheer terror you are experiencing. For them, it's just a regular day and another frustratingly slow line at the grocery store.

You realize you are out of options. It's time to run. You excuse yourself from the line looking embarrassed as it is now that it is your turn to pay. The cashier looks bewildered when you leave your shopping behind and stroll towards the door.

There is no time for excuses - you need to be alone. You leave the supermarket and get into your car to ride it out alone. You wonder whether or not this one was the big one. The one you fear will push you over the edge mentally and physically. Ten minutes later the panic subsides. It's only 11:00 in the morning, how in the world can you make it through the rest of your day?

If you suffer from panic or anxiety attacks, the above scenario probably sounds very familiar. It may have even induced feelings of anxiety and panic just reading it. In fact, it was difficult for me just to write it.

The particular situations that trigger your panic and anxiety may differ. Maybe the bodily sensations are a little different. What's important to realize is that panic attacks are very real to the people who are having them and they should never be pushed off to the side.

I remember one evening at home when I was by myself watching one of my favorite television programs. I thought I was in a safe place. There was no obvious trigger and I felt completely relaxed. Out of nowhere, I began having symptoms of a panic attack. The four walls of my living room were closing in around me. I couldn't breathe and felt like I was dying.

I stepped out on my front porch for some fresh air and began deep breathing exercises. The symptoms eventually went away, but it left me wondering why exactly I had that attack. There was no obvious reason, no stressful situation, and no indicator that a panic attack might be impending.

That's the strange thing about panic. Sometimes your mind can play tricks on you. Even when you think you're in no danger of having a panic attack, your brain might be feeling differently. That's the scary part. The good part is that there are ways you can combat panic attacks and cope much better when you find yourself in that situation.

DEALING WITH PANIC ATTACKS

If you have panic attacks, it may help to comfort you that you are not alone! You're not even one in a million. In America, it is estimated that almost 5% of the population suffer from some form of anxiety disorder.

For some, it may be the infrequent panic attacks that only crop up in particular situations-like when having to speak in front of others, while, for other people, it can be so frequent and recurring that it inhibits them from leaving their home. Frequent panic attacks often develop into what medical physicians refer to as an "anxiety disorder."

There are many ways of coping with an anxiety disorder. Some may not work for you, but others just might. It helps to know some of the most common coping techniques for dealing with panic attacks when they begin.

Your first step is to recognize when a panic attack is about to begin. When you have enough of them, you start to really pay attention to the tingling sensation, the shortness of breath, and the disconnection from the real life around you.

Many people I talk to wonder what that disconnection is like. They have a hard time understanding it. Those of us who have panic attacks are all too familiar with it. It's like you can look at a solid object and see that it is there. You know it's there, but a part of your mind doubts that it really IS there.

You may find yourself reaching out to touch that object just to be sure. You feel like you're not a part of the world around you. It's as if you are just a spectator in your own life with no control over anything around you. This is a horrible feeling.

How do you start trying to combat your panic attacks? What if I told you the trick to ending panic and anxiety attacks is to WANT to have one. That sounds strange, even contradictory, doesn't it? But the want really does help push it away.

Does this mean that you should be able to bring on a panic attack at this very moment? Absolutely not! What it means is that when you are afraid of something – in this case a panic attack – it will more than likely appear and wreak havoc. When you stand up to the attack, your chances of fending it off are much greater.

If you resist a situation out of fear, the fear around that issue will persist. How do you stop resisting–you move directly into it, into the path of the anxiety, and by doing so it cannot persist.

In essence what this means is that if you daily voluntarily seek to have a panic attack, you cannot have one. Try in this very moment to have a panic attack and I will guarantee you cannot. You may not realize it but you have always decided to panic. You make the choice by saying this is beyond my control whether it be consciously or sub-consciously.

Another way to appreciate this is to imagine having a panic attack as like standing on a cliff's edge. The anxiety seemingly pushes you closer to falling over the edge. To be rid of the fear you must metaphorically jump. You must jump off the cliff edge and into the anxiety and fear and all the things that you fear most.

How do you jump? You jump by wanting to have a panic attack. Your real safety is the fact that a panic attack will never harm you. That is a medical fact.

Anxiety causes an imbalance in your life whereby all of the mental worry creates a top-heavy sensation. All of your focus is moved from the center of your body to the head. Schools of meditation often like to demonstrate an example of this top-heavy imbalance by showing how easily the body can lose its sense of center.

The key to overcoming panic attacks is to relax. That's easy to say but difficult to do. A good way to do this is to concentrate on your breathing making sure it is slow and steady. One of the first signs of a panic attack is difficulty breathing, and you may find yourself panting to catch a breath. When you focus on making those breaths even, your heart rate will slow down and the panic will subside.

Breathing more slowly and deeply has a calming effect. A good way to breathe easier is to let all the air out of your lungs. This forces your lungs to reach for a deeper breath next time. Continue to focus on your out-breath, letting all the air out of your lungs and soon you'll find your breathing is deeper and you feel calmer.

Ideally, you want to take the focus off the fact that you are having a panic attack. Try to press your feet, one at a time, into the ground. Feel how connected and rooted they are to the ground.

An even better way is to lie down with your bottom near a wall. Place your feet against the wall (your knees are bent) and press your feet one at a time into the wall. If you can breathe in as you press your foot against the wall, and breathe out as you release it, it will be more effective. You should alternate between your feet. Do this for 10 - 15 minutes or until the panic subsides.

Use all of your senses to take full notice of what you see, hear, feel, and smell in your environment. This will help you to remain present. Panic is generally associated with remembering upsetting events from the past or anticipating something upsetting in the future. Anything that helps keep you focused in the present will be calming. Try holding a pet; looking around your room and noticing the colors, textures, and shapes; listening closely to the sounds you hear; call a friend; or smell the smells that are near you.

Many people strongly advocate aromatherapy to deal with panic and anxiety. Lavender can have an especially calming and soothing effect when you smell it. You can find essential oil of lavender at many stores. Keep it handy and take a sniff when you start feeling anxious.

Try putting a few drops of lavender essence oil into some oil (olive or grape seed oil will do) and rub on your body. Keep a prepared mixture in a dark glass bottle for when you need it. You can even prepare several bottles, with a small one to carry with you.

Other essential oils known to help panic and panic attacks are helichrysum, frankincense, and marjoram. Smell each of them, and use what smells best to you, or a combination of your favorite oils mixed in olive or grape seed oil.

You may want to prepare yourself BEFORE a panic attack happens. When you're not in a panicked state, make a list of the things that you're afraid will happen. Then write out calming things that tell you the opposite of your fears. Then you can repeat these things to yourself when the panic starts to come.

Prepare a list of things to do in case of panicked feelings, and it will be ready for you when you need it. Fill it with lots of soothing messages and ideas of calming things to do. I find this to be a very helpful tool. I am never without my small notebook that has these positive affirmations in it.

Panic can be a very scary thing to go through, especially if you're alone. Preparing for when the panic comes can really help reduce the panic, and even sometimes help to prevent it.

Another great tool to combating anxiety and stress is to use visualization.

CALM YOURSELF WITH VISUALIZATION

The purpose of visualization is to enable you to quickly clear mental stress, tension, and anxious thinking. The visualization can be used when feeling stressed and is particularly useful when your mind is racing with fearful, anxious thinking.

This visualization process, when practiced frequently, is very effective for eliminating deep-seated mental anxieties or intrusive thoughts. To gain maximum benefit, the exercise must be carried out for longer then 10 minutes at a time, as anything shorter will not bring noticeable results.

There is no right or wrong way to carry out the visualization. Be intuitive with it and do not feel you are unable to carry it out if you feel you are not very good at seeing mental imagery. As long as your attention is on the exercise, you will gain benefit.

It is best to do this exercise in a quiet place where you won't be disturbed, and then when you are more practiced you will be able to get the same positive results in a busier environment such as the workplace. You should notice a calming effect on your state of mind along with a sensation of mental release and relaxation.

Either sitting or standing, close your eyes and move your attention to your breath. To become aware of your breathing, place one hand on your upper chest and one on your stomach. Take a breath and let your stomach swell forward as you breathe in and fall back gently as you breathe out. Take the same depth of breath each time and try to get a steady rhythm going.

Your hand on your chest should have little or no movement. Again, try to take the same depth of breath each time you breathe in. This is called Diaphragmatic Breathing.

When you feel comfortable with this technique, try to slow your breathing rate down by instituting a short pause after you have breathed out and before you breathe in again. Initially, it may feel as though you are not getting enough air in, but with regular practice this slower rate will soon start to feel comfortable.

It is often helpful to develop a cycle where you count to three when you breathe in, pause, and then count to three when you breathe out (or 2, or 4 - whatever is comfortable for you). This will also help you focus on your breathing without any other thoughts coming into your mind.

If you are aware of other thoughts entering your mind, just let them go and bring your attention back to counting and breathing. Continue doing this for a few minutes. If you practice this, you will begin to strengthen the Diaphragmatic Muscle, and it will start to work normally, leaving you with a nice relaxed feeling all the time.

Now move your attention to your feet. Try to really feel your feet. See if you can feel each toe. Picture the base of your feet and visualize roots growing slowly out through your soles and down into the earth. The roots are growing with quickening pace and are reaching deep into the soil of the earth. You are now rooted firmly to the earth and feel stable like a large oak or redwood tree.

Stay with this feeling of grounded safety and security for a few moments. Once you have created a strong feeling or impression of being grounded like a tree, visualize a cloud of bright light forming way above you. A bolt of lightning from the luminous cloud hits the crown of your head, and that ignites a band of bright white light descending slowly from your head all the way down your body, over your legs, and out past your toes.

As the band of light passes over you, feel it clearing your mental state. It is illuminating your mind and clearing any disturbing or stressful thoughts that you may have been thinking about. Repeat this image four or five times until you feel a sense of clearing and release from any anxious thinking.

In finishing, see yourself standing under a large, luminescent waterfall. The water is radiant and bubbling with vitality and life. As you stand under the waterfall, you can feel the water run over every inch of your body, soothing you and instilling within you a sense of deep calm.

Try to taste the water. Open your mouth and let it run into your mouth, refreshing you. Hear it as it bounces off the ground around you. The water is life itself and it is washing away stress and worry from your mind and body. After a moment, open your eyes.

Try to use all of your senses when carrying out the visualization. To make the pictures in your mind as real as possible, use your senses of touch, taste, and hearing. Feel the water trickle down your body; hear the sound it makes as it splashes over you.

The more realistic the imagined scenarios, the more benefit you will gain. Many people report very beneficial and soothing results from using these simple visualizations frequently. The mind is much like a muscle in that, in order to relax, it needs to regularly release what it is holding onto.

You can use any situation or location that will help calm you. We liken this to "finding your happy place". Maybe you feel relaxed in a swimming pool or on the beach. Imagine yourself there. Just make sure wherever you go in your mind is a place where you can be calm and rested.

By visualizing the different situations, you are allowing your mind to release. It is like sending a message to your brain that when you close your eyes and begin this process it is time for letting go of anything that it has been mentally holding onto, including anxious thinking.

In order to train your mind how to let go of the stress, it is important to practice this daily. With practice, you can learn to release all stress within minutes of starting the exercise. Your daily practice should take place before going to bed, as that will enable you to sleep more soundly.

Many people do not do these visualizations in the bedroom but some other room before going to bed. That way, when they enter the bedroom and close the door, they are leaving the mental stress and anxious thinking behind them. Just be sure you have the opportunity to totally concentrate on your mental images.

Visualization as a tool for dealing with mental stress is very effective. If such visualization is carried out properly, you can reach a deep feeling of inner calm. This technique probably will not work in helping to end an anxiety attack, but it can help that attack from beginning. It is a very powerful support tool for ridding yourself of general anxiety sensations.

With practice, you find you go days without having anxious thinking interrupt your life, and importantly, this significantly reduces the level of general anxiety you feel.

Visualization is a tool you can use to overcome anxious thoughts and feelings. Let's look at various ways that you can combat excessive stress – beginning with music.

USING MUSIC TO BEAT STRESS

Listening to music will also alleviate stress. Everyone has different tastes in music. You should listen to the music that makes you feel comfortable. Sitting down and forcing yourself to listen to relaxation music that you don't like may create stress, not alleviate it. Music is a significant mood-changer and reliever of stress, working on many levels at once.

The entire human energetic system is extremely influenced by sounds, the physical body and charka centers respond specifically to certain tones and frequencies. Special consideration should be given to the positive effects of one actually playing or creating music themselves.

Among the first stress-fighting changes that take place when we hear a tune is an increase in deep breathing. The body's production of serotonin also accelerates.

Playing music in the background while you are working has been found to reduce the stress of the workplace. Music was found to reduce heart rates and to promote higher body temperature - an indication of the onset of relaxation. Combining music with relaxation therapy was more effective than doing relaxation therapy alone.

Many experts suggest that it is the rhythm of the music or the beat that has the calming effect on us although we may not be very conscious about it. When in our mother's womb, we were influenced by the heartbeat of our mother. We respond to the soothing music at later stages in life, perhaps associating it with the safe, relaxing, protective environment provided by our mother.

Music can be one of the most soothing or nerve-wracking experiences available. Choosing what will work for any individual is difficult, most will choose something they 'like' instead of what might be beneficial.

In doing extensive research on what any given piece of music produces in the physiological response system many unexpected things were found. Many of the so-called meditation and relaxation recordings actually produced adverse EEG patterns, just as bad as Hard Rock and Heavy Metal.

The surprising thing was many selections of Celtic, Native American as well as various music containing loud drums or flutes were extremely soothing. The most profound finding was any music performed live and even at moderately loud volumes even if it was somewhat discordant had very a beneficial response.

As we mentioned before, no single music is a good fit for everyone. People have different tastes. It is important that you like the music being played. I recently picked up a rest and relaxation CD that has done wonders for me. It has the sounds of the ocean in the background while beautiful piano music plays. I find this very soothing.

It's not a good idea to play ballads or songs that remind you of a sad time in your life when you're trying to de-stress. You're trying to relax and wash away the anxious thoughts. The last thing that you need is for a sad song to bring back unhappy memories.

Here are some general guidelines to follow when using music to de-stress.

- To wash away stress, try taking a 20-minute "sound bath." Put some relaxing music on, then lie in a comfortable position on a couch or on the floor near the speakers. For a deeper experience, you can wear headphones to focus your attention and to avoid distraction.

- Choose music with a slow rhythm - slower than the natural heartbeat, which is about 72 beats per minute. Music that has repeating or cyclical pattern is found to be effective in most people.

- As the music plays, allow it to wash over you, rinsing off the stress from the day. Focus on your breathing, letting it deepen, slow and become regular. Concentrate on the silence between the notes in the music; this keeps you from analyzing the music and makes relaxation more complete.

- If you need stimulation after a day of work, go for a faster music rather than slow calming music. Turn up the volume and DANCE! It doesn't matter if you can actually dance. Just move along with the music and do what feels good. You'll be shocked at the release you can feel!

- When going gets tough, go for a music you are familiar with - such as a childhood favorite or favorite oldies. Familiarity often breeds calmness.

- Take walks with your favorite music playing on your I Pod or MP3 Player. Inhale and exhale in tune with the music. Let the music take you. Combining exercise, imagery and music is a fantastic stress reliever.

- Listening to the sounds of nature, such as ocean waves or the calm of a deep forest, can reduce stress. Try taking a 15 to 20 minute walk if you're near the seashore or a quiet patch of woods. If not, you can buy tapes of these sounds in many music stores.

Another great relaxation technique is self-hypnosis.

SELF-HYPNOSIS FOR STRESS

You can also practice self-hypnosis on your own. Find a quiet place where you can fully relax and listen to your inner voice. Don't try to make something happen, just let your mind listen and relax. A large part of achieving a hypnotic state is to allow it to happen naturally.

Don't watch for certain signs or signals that you might be in a hypnotic state. If you look for these signs, you won't be able to fully relax and gain the benefits of self-hypnosis.

There are lots of different ways to experience hypnosis. Although, no two people will have exactly the same experience, everyone will find the hypnotic state pleasant. There are no "bad trips" in hypnosis. Keep in mind that self-hypnosis is a skill, and that you will continue to get better at it. The more experienced you become the more powerful self hypnosis is.

Set up a schedule of practice, allowing yourself between 10 and 30 minutes of uninterrupted time. If possible, practice during the best part of your day, at a time when you are least likely to be disturbed by others.

Most people find it best to practice lying down, in a comfortable position, with as few distractions as possible. If you are bothered by noise while you practice you can try to block it out with some other source of sound.

You can try stereo music in the background, or white noise if you like. If like most people you don't have a white noise generator, try tuning a radio receiver between stations. The static you get when you do that is similar to white noise. However this takes an older or cheaper FM receiver without a noise suppressor. Sometimes AM tuners can be used for this. This should just be in the background and not too loud to be distracting.

The basic divisions of a hypnotic induction are relaxation, deepening, suggestion application, and termination.

1. Relaxation

Your first job in the hypnotic induction is to slow the juices down and get yourself relaxed. But don't try to force your mind to relax. If you get yourself physically relaxed, your mind will follow.

Relaxation – really deep relaxation – is an ability that most people have either lost or never developed. Some people can do it quite easily, though. They just let go of their tensions and let every part of their body become limp and relaxed. If you are one of these people, begin your self-hypnosis practice by getting nicely relaxed. Take your time. This is not something you want to rush.

The time involved for the relaxation phase of your self-hypnosis induction can vary from half an hour to just a few seconds. It is an important part of the induction and should not be slighted. As you get better and your skill increases you will recognize deeply relaxed states, and you will be able to achieve them in a surprisingly short time. But as a beginner, take your time. It will be time well spent.

A very popular method of deep relaxation is the Jacobson Progressive Relaxation procedure. This involves tensing each of the major muscle groups of your body (foot and lower leg on each side, upper leg and hip, abdomen, etc.). Tense the muscle group for a few seconds, then let go.

2. Deepening Procedures

Once you have completed the relaxation phase of your self-hypnosis induction procedure, you can begin to deepen the relaxed state. At some time between the deep relaxation and the deepening procedures you will move into a hypnotic state. You probably won't know it, especially as a beginner, but it will happen sooner or later.

One of the first hurdles a beginner must get over is the compulsion to "watch for it." That is, you will keep waiting for hypnosis to happen, for some change in your awareness or the way you feel that will say to you, "You're hypnotized."

Watching for hypnosis will definitely get in your way if you don't get it out of your mind. Going into a hypnotic state is, in this respect, similar to going to sleep. If you try to catch yourself going to sleep – if you try to be aware of the precise instant in which you actually go to sleep – you are much less likely to go to sleep. "Watching" keeps you awake.

In this same way you will not know when you go into a hypnotic state (but that won't be because you lost consciousness – you won't). Later, after you have been practicing regularly for a few weeks or a month or two, you'll be much more familiar with yourself and how it feels to be hypnotized.

Does it take everyone weeks or even months to get into a good hypnotic state? Definitely not. Some people have an amazing experience the very first time they try it. Others might practice for several days, noticing nothing, and then suddenly they have one of those great induction sessions in which they know something stupendously good happened. But if you're not one of those people, don't worry about it. Just keep practicing and you will eventually get there.

One of the most popular deepening procedures is the countdown technique. Hollywood also likes this one. That is why you see it in so many movies. That and the swinging watch.

To use the countdown technique you simply start counting downward from, say, 20 (or 100, or whatever). Adjust the countdown number to what feels right to you after you have practiced a few times. Imagine that you are drifting deeper with each count. Other images and thoughts will probably intrude themselves as you count. That is natural. Just gently brush them aside, continuing with your counting.

The speed with which you count down should be natural; not too fast, not too slow. For most people this means counting at a rate of about one count for each two or three seconds. Do it at a rate that feels comfortable and relaxed to you. Some people like to tie the count with their breathing. As they drift deeper their breathing slows down, so their counting also slows down.

Don't count out loud; just think your way down the count. You want to avoid as much physical involvement and movement as possible.

3. Suggestion Application in self-hypnosis

Once you have reached the end of your deepening procedure you are ready to apply suggestions. What you have done during the relaxation and deepening procedures is increase your suggestibility. That is, you have opened up your subconscious mind at least a little bit to receive your suggestions. This works because of the particular, and peculiar, characteristics of the subconscious part of your mind.

The most common and easiest way to apply suggestions is to have them worked out ahead of time, properly prepared, worded, and memorized. It should not be too difficult to remember them because they should be rather short and you are the one who composed them. If you have them ready and remembered, you can simply think your way through them at this point.

Dialogue, or more properly monologue, is also okay. You just talk inside your head, to yourself about what it is you want to do, be, become, whatever.

Don't say you. This is about you, so make sure when you think you doin it in the first person, for example, "I am eating less and becoming more slender every day."

Elaborated suggestions are generally wordier and more of an ad-lib: "Food is becoming less important to me every day and I am filling my time with more important and meaningful pursuits than eating. It is getting easier and easier to pass up desserts and other fattening foods . . ." and so on.

Generally speaking, the most effective kind of suggestion is image suggestion. Image suggestions usually do not use language at all. You can liken this to seeing yourself in a calm, relaxed state while in the middle of a chaotic situation. Actually see yourself in your mind's eye.

Although people sometimes see immediate results from their suggestions, it is more likely to take a little time for them to kick in. So don't be impatient. On the other hand, if you have not begun to see some results within, say, a couple of weeks, you need to change your suggestions.

4. Termination

Once you have finished applying suggestions you can terminate your session. You could just open your eyes, get up and go about your business, but that is not a good idea.

You should formally identify the end of every session. By doing this you provide a clear boundary between the hypnotic state and your ordinary conscious awareness. A clear termination also prevents your self-hypnosis practice session from turning into a nap. If you want to take a nap, take a nap. But don't do it in a way that sleeping becomes associated with self-hypnosis practice.

If you are practicing at bedtime and don't care if you go on to sleep, that is okay. But still draw the line in your mind to indicate the end of your self-hypnosis session.

To terminate the session, think to yourself that you are going to be fully awake and alert after you count up to three. "One, I'm beginning to come out of it, moving toward a waking state. Two, I'm becoming more alert, getting ready to wake up. Three, I'm completely awake." Self-hypnosis can work wonders when it is practiced on a regular basis. You'd be amazingly surprised at the level of relaxation you can get to.

Now we'll move onto stress management techniques.

STRESS MANAGEMENT

We know that stress is a part of life and there's no getting away from it. In fact, some stress is good stress. It can motivate you to do things you would not do in a relaxed state. Stress can make you brave enough to go forward when normally you would hesitate.

You have to be resilient in order to effectively cope with stress and help it enhance your life instead of control it. How do you get strong and resilient? By learning how to take control of your stress and make it work FOR you instead of AGAINST you.

Recognizing stress symptoms can be a positive influence in that we're compelled to take action – and the sooner the better. It's not always easy to discern why you have the stress in each situation but some of the more common events that trigger those emotions are the death of a loved one, the birth of a child, a job promotion, or a new relationship. We experience stress when we readjust our lives. Your body is asking for your help when you feel these stress symptoms.

There are three major approaches to manage stress. The first is the action-oriented approach. In this method, the problems that cause stress are identified and necessary changes are made alleviate them.

The next approach is emotionally-oriented. Where you overcome stress by giving a different color to the experience that caused stress. The situation, which causes stress, is seen humorously or from a different angle. Sometimes you can't avoid the stressor but you can learn to see the humor instead of the doom.

The third way is acceptance-oriented approach. This approach focuses on surviving the stress caused due to some problem in the past.

The first stress management tip is to understand the root cause of your stress. No one understands your problem better than you do. A few minutes spend to recognize your true feelings can completely change the situation.

During this process, identify what triggered the stress. Share this with a loved one if you can. If you are overstressed and feel you are going to collapse, take a deep breath and count to ten. This pumps extra oxygen into your system and rejuvenates the entire body.

When under severe stress meditate for a moment and pull out of the current situation for a little while. Stand up from your current position and walk. Stretch yourself. Soon you will find that the stress has lessened.

This is because you have relaxed. Relaxation is the best medicine for stress. Smiling is another form of stress management. If you are at the work place, just stand up and smile at your colleague in the far corner. You will see a change in your mood.

You can also invent your own stress management tips. The basic idea is to identify the cause of stress and to pull out from it for a moment and then deal with it. Taking a short walk and look at nature can be another stress reliever. Drinking a glass of water or playing small games are simple stress management techniques. The whole idea is change the focus of attention. Then when you return to the problem, it does not look as monstrous.

Here are five quick steps you can take toward relieving stress:

1. Don't just sit there. Move! According to many psychologists, motion creates emotion. When you are idle, it's

easier to become depressed. Your heart rate slows down, less oxygen travels to your brain, and you are slumped somewhere in a chair blocking air from reaching your lungs.

Right now, regardless of how you are feeling, get up and walk around at a fast tempo. Even jump up and down a little bit. It may sound silly but the results speak for themselves. Try it for a few minutes. It works like magic.

Exercise can be a great stress buster. People with anxiety disorders might worry that aerobic exercise could bring on a panic attack. After all, when you exercise, your heart rate goes up, you begin to sweat, and your breathing becomes heavier.

Don't panic – it's not an attack! Tell yourself this over and over while you're exercising. Realize that there's a big difference between the physical side of exercise and what happens when you exercise.

2. Smell the roses. Go on that trip you've been dreaming about. Visit an old friend. Paint a picture. Just do something for yourself. It'll jolt your imagination and spur your creativity and help you detach from your daily routine.

3. Help others cope with their problems. It is very therapeutic when you engross yourself in helping others. You will be surprised how many people's problems are worse than

yours. You can offer others assistance in countless ways. Don't curl up in your bed and let depression take hold of you.

Get out and help somebody. But be careful. Don't get caught up in other people's problems in an attempt to forget about your own.

4. Laugh a little. You've heard that laughter is a good internal medicine. It relieves tension and loosens the muscles. It causes blood to flow to the heart and brain. More importantly, laughter releases a chemical that rids the body of pains.

Every day, researchers discover new benefits of laughter. Let me ask you this question: "Can you use a good dose of belly-shaking laughter every now and then?" Of course you can. What you are waiting for? Go a comedy club or rent some funny movies.

5. Wear your knees out. If there were one sustainable remedy I could offer you when the going gets tough, it would be prayer. Many people, depending on their faith, might call it meditation. It doesn't matter what you call it, as long as you have a place to run to.

6. Make stress your friend

Acknowledge that stress is good and make stress your friend! Based on the body's natural "fight or flight" response that burst of energy will enhance your performance at the right moment. Top sportsmen are not relaxed before a big competition. Use stress wisely to push yourself that little bit harder when it counts most.

7. Stress is contagious

What we mean by this is that negative people can be a huge stressor. Negativity breeds stress and some people do nothing but complain. Don't get caught up in their downing behavior. Recognize that these kinds of people have their own stress and then limit your contact with them. You can try to play stress doctor and teach them how to better manage their stress, but be aware that this may contribute more to your own stress, so tread lightly.

8. Copy good stress managers

When people around you are losing their heads, watch for who keeps calm. What are they doing differently? What is their attitude? What language do they use? Are they trained and experienced?

Figure it out from afar or sit them down for a chat. Learn from the best stress managers and copy what they do.

9. Use heavy breathing

You can trick your body into relaxing by using heavy breathing. Breathe in slowly for a count of 7 then breathe out for a count of 11. Repeat the 7-11 breathing until your heart rate slows down, your sweaty palms dry off and things start to feel more normal.

10. Stop stress thought trains

It is possible to tangle yourself up in a stress knot all by yourself. If you're constantly expecting the worst to happen and say negative things to yourself. For example, "If this happens, then that might happen and then we're all up the creek!" Most bad things never happen, so don't waste all that energy worrying needlessly. Give stress thought-trains the red light and stop them in their tracks.

11. Know your stress hot spots and trigger points

Presentations, interviews, meetings, giving difficult feedback, tight deadlines. These are all things that can get your heart racing.

Make your own list of stress trigger points or hot spots. Be specific. Is it only presentations to a certain audience that get you worked up? Does one project cause more stress than another? Did you drink too much coffee? Knowing what causes your stress is powerful information, as you can take action to make it less stressful.

12. Eat, drink, sleep and be merry!

Lack of sleep, poor diet and no exercise wreaks havoc on our body and mind. Kind of obvious, but worth mentioning as it's often ignored as a stress management technique. Listen to what your mother used to say and don't burn the candle at both ends!

Avoid using artificial means to dealing with your stress. That means don't automatically pour a glass of wine when you think you're getting stressed out and don't light up a cigarette. In actuality, alcohol, nicotine, caffeine, and drugs can make the problem worse. A better idea is to practice the relaxation techniques you've learned here. Then, once you're relaxed, you can have that glass of wine if you want.

13. Go outside and enjoy Mother Nature. A little sunshine and activity can have amazing ramifications on your stress level and will enhance your entire outlook towards life. Your improved attitude will have a positive effect on everyone in your family and your circle of friends. Things that once seemed overwhelming will soon become trivial matters, causing you to wonder what the predicament was.

Not only will you be less stressed, you will be healthier, happier, and more energetic; ready to face whatever obstacles come your way.

14. Give yourself permission to be a 'kid' again. Be carefree and creative. Allow yourself freedom to express yourself and don't worry that you're not keeping with the image of who you

are 'supposed' to be. Just relax and enjoy yourself. We all have an inner child, let it free.

15. Don't set unrealistic for goals for yourself. Many people set themselves up for defeat simply by setting unrealistic goals. Whatever your goal is allow sufficient time to reach it and realize that setbacks will probably happen.

16. Learn it is OK to say 'no' occasionally. Many people feel that they have to say 'yes' to everyone. You can't be all things to all people. You must first meet your own needs before you can give to others.

17. Make time for yourself, your number one priority; once your own needs are met you will find you have more time for others. And you may find more pleasure in helping others when you don't feel that you must always put others needs before your own.

18. This is a great idea that works. Ok ready, now ... YELL! That's right, scream at the top of your lungs – as loud as you can. While this may not be feasible in your home, it works great when you're in your car with the windows rolled up. Let out a guttural yelp from deep down inside. It's liberating!

19. Sing. Music is extremely beneficial to rid yourself of stress. Think how much better you can feel when you belt out

"Copacabana" at the top of your lungs! Who cares if you can't carry a tune? You're doing this for you!

20. Take up a new hobby like knitting or crocheting. Don't worry about being good at it. It's the process that's beneficial. Sitting still while performing repetitive movements is calming and stabilizing for many people. It can be time to collect your thoughts.

21. Start a garden. Even apartment-dwellers can do this. Inside in pots, pots on the patio, pots, a small spot in your yard. There is a little work to setting it up.

Tending plants, fruits, vegetables, flowers and watching them grow, bloom, or yield food is rewarding. Avid gardeners say working a garden is the best way to control stress and worry. An added benefit is the creation of a more beautiful, restful environment.

22. Play with a dog or cat. Experts say pet owners have longer lives and fewer stress symptoms that non-pet owners. Playing with your pet provide good vibrations – for you and for the pet! It's a form of social interaction with no pressure to meet anyone's expectations!

23. Look at the stars and the moon. It can be a very humbling experience to lay on a blanket with your hands behind

your head and gaze up into the night sky. It's more than humbling; it's downright beautiful and relaxing!

24. Treat yourself to some comfort food. But be careful or over-eating could become your big stressor. Enjoy in moderation and you'll feel better.

25. Swing. Remember the feeling of sitting inside that little piece of leather on the playground as you sway back and forth and feel the wind whipping through you hair? Do that! If you don't have a swing in your yard, go to a playground and remember to pump your legs back and forth to see how high you can go.

26. Take a candle lit bubble bath. Even men will benefit from a warm bath bathed in the soft glow of candlelight. Lay your head back, feel the bubbles and the warm water, and let your stress go right down the drain.

Now you have twenty-six ways to relax and de-stress! You can come up with your own ways as well! The key, really, is to find something that makes you feel better when you are overwhelmed and practice that method faithfully. You'll be a healthier person overall.

JUST SAY NO!

This is a big issue so let's look at it more closely. A huge problem people who are overly stressed have is the ability to say "No". Maybe your mother wants you to take Grandma to the store, but you're in the middle of a big work project. Perhaps your best friend asks if you wouldn't mind babysitting her kids when you've already made plans with yourself to get a haircut.

There's no reason why you have to say "Yes" to everyone. In fact, there are often many times when you should turn them down. If you find yourself agreeing to do things when you really don't want to, you're a people pleaser. Sounds like a nice trait to have, but it is a huge stressor.

People pleasers think of other people's needs before their own. They worry about what other people want, think, or need, and spend a lot of time doing things for others. They rarely do things for themselves, and feel guilty when they do. It's hard work being a people pleaser.

People pleasers hold back from saying what they really think. They don't ask for the things they would like if they think someone will be upset with them for it. Yet they often spend time with people who don't consider their needs at all. In fact, people pleasers often feel driven to make insensitive or unhappy people feel better - even at the detriment to themselves.

Constantly trying to please other people is draining and many people pleasers feel anxious, worried, unhappy, and tired a lot of the time. They may not understand why no one does anything for them, when they do so much for others and yet they don't ask for what they need.

A people pleaser may believe that if they ask someone for help and that person agrees, that person would be giving out of obligation, not because they really wanted to. The thinking goes - if they really wanted to help, they would have offered without my asking.

This line of thinking happens because people pleasers themselves feel obliged to help and do not always do things because they want to. Sadly, people pleasers have been taught that their worth depends on doing things for others.

When they do take a moment for themselves, they feel selfish, indulgent, and guilty which is why they are often on the go, rushing to get things done. Since people pleasers accomplish so much and are easy to get along with, they are often the first to be asked to do things - they are vulnerable to be being taken advantage of.

People pleasers were most likely raised in homes where their needs and feelings were not valued, respected, or considered important. They were often expected as children to respond to or to take care of other people's needs. Or they may have been silenced, neglected, or otherwise abused, thus learning that their feelings and needs were not important.

In many cultures, girls are raised to be people pleasers - to think of others' needs first, and to neglect their own. Most women have at least some degree of people pleasing in them. Men who identified with their mothers often do as well.

People pleasers' focus is mostly on others and away from themselves. They often feel empty, or don't know how they feel, what they think, or what they want for themselves. It's possible to change this pattern, starting now.

First, practice saying NO. This is a very important word! Say it as often as you can, just to hear the word come out of your mouth. Say it out loud when you are alone. Practice phrases with NO in them, such as, "No, I can't do that" or "No, I don't want to go there". Try it for simple things first, and then build your way up to harder situations.

Stop saying YES all the time. Try to pause or take a breath before responding to someone's request. You may want to answer requests with "I need to think about it first, I'll get back to you" or "Let me check my schedule and call you back". Use any phrase that you feel comfortable with that gives you time before you automatically respond with YES.

You will feel guilty when you start this but it won't always be so. Remember that your mental health is well worth the aggravation you may have to take from others. What's important is you.

Figure out what gives you pleasure. For example, you may like reading magazines, watching videos, going to a park, or listening to music. Give yourself permission to do those things and then enjoy them.

Ask someone to help you with something. I know this is a hard one but you can do it! After all, everyone else is asking YOU for favors. Be tolerant if they turn you down. Just because you have always told them "Yes" doesn't mean they always have to tell you "Yes".

Many people pleasers believe that nobody will like them if they stop doing things for other people. If this happens than you were being used and it's better that they aren't in your life anyway. People enjoy your company for who you are and not for what you do. You deserve to take time to yourself, to say NO, and to take care of yourself without feeling guilty. It's within your reach to change - one small step at a time!

TAKE A BREAK

So often, we know inside ourselves that we need a break. That break might be a full-fledged vacation or a weekend getaway. Either way, getting out of the daily grind can be amazingly liberating and a huge way to get rid of stress and anxiety.

Unfortunately, many people think they can't take the time to get away. This is toxic thinking. Get out and get away!

How many times have you continued working, knowing that you are not giving 100% to the task at hand? How many times have you read or written the same sentence over and over again, as your mind keeps wandering and thinking about other things? How often have you wanted to take a break from the family or kids but feared the consequences of doing so? It's time for a break!

Why do we not allow ourselves the time to take a 'time out'? Perhaps we feel like we don't deserve it or that there's just too much to be done. There are many genuine reasons for needing to complete jobs and tasks; however we may also on occasion have 'hidden agendas' as to why we cannot stop for a break. Why?

Ego - some people enjoy boasting about, 'how late they had to work in order to complete a project' or 'how much effort they invested in order to complete the job so quickly'. This type of person is often looking to impress others with their efforts, thereby increasing their ego in the process.

Or perhaps you think that you can't take the time off. "I can't stop; I just have to get this finished". Does this sound familiar? "I can't stop because the job has to be finished, WHY? So I can move straight on to the next thing, and the next, and the next etc..." This person will find that there is always something that has to be done, which will constantly prevent him/her from taking a break.

You feel like you need to be needed. A mother managing the household, kids and other chores may feel as if her household will collapse if she were to put her feet up or take a weekend off! By not taking a break she can keep convincing herself that her role is crucial and the family would collapse without her. This may be true, but it won't happen because she's taken a time out for herself.

Get rid of that thinking! You can get some amazing benefits just by taking a little time for yourself! Allowing your mind and/or body to rest can help re-focus your attention, sharpen your wits and increase motivation. In addition, taking time out helps to relieve stress, can aid the recovery of tired muscles and also promotes the discovery that there is more to life than just work.

Many athletes will tell you that an important part of their training routine is rest. Muscles need time to repair after a workout. Remember that your brain is a muscle too. It needs time to rest and recuperate in order to perform at its best. By giving your brain time off, you'll be able to better concentrate. Tasks that you once struggled with will be easier. A break can be anything from a 10-minute meditation session to a trip around the world, and anything in-between. A break needs to take your mind off the everyday tedium of life.

When you take this rest, you absolutely can not feel guilty about it. You need this time off, so enjoy it. You'll be a better mother, father, wife or husband for it.

If you're feeling tired, unmotivated or just in need of a rest, don't be a martyr or look negatively at this. You may actually find that in reality, allowing yourself a break will actually help you ultimately become more efficient and effective in every part of your life. Plus you'll get the badly needed recharging of your "batteries" that you need and sorely deserve!

Work can probably be one of the most stressful places to be. You might think that none of these techniques can help you when you're around your co-workers. You couldn't be more wrong.

RELAXING AT WORK

Some of the suggestions in this book can certainly be practiced at work. Here's a tried and true method to help you relax at work.

First and foremost, find a place to sit. Sit up straight with your back against the back of your chair, your feet flat on the floor, and your hands resting lightly on your thighs.

If possible, close your eyes. You may do the exercise without closing your eyes, but closing your eyes will help you relax a bit more. Do not clench your eyes shut. Let your eyelids fall naturally.

Breathe in slowly through your nose, counting to 5. Hold the breath for a count of 5. Breathe out slowly, counting to five. Repeat.

This exercise is performed by tensing and holding a set of muscles for a count of 5, and then relaxing the set of muscles for a count of 5.

When you tense each muscle set, do it as hard as you can without hurting yourself. When you release the hold, be as relaxed as possible.

Begin by tensing your feet. Do this by pulling your feet off the floor and your toes toward you while keeping your heels on the floor. Hold for a slow count of 5. Release the hold. Let your feet fall gently back. Feel the relaxation. Think about how it feels compared to when you tensed the muscles. Relax for a count of 5.

Next tense your thigh muscles as hard as you can. Hold for a count of 5. Relax the muscles and count to 5.

Tighten your abdominal muscles and hold for a count of 5. Relax the muscles for a count of 5. Be sure you are continuing to sit up straight.

Tense your arm and hand muscles by squeezing your hands into fists as hard as you can. Hold for a count of 5. Relax the muscles completely for a count of 5.

Tighten your upper back by pushing your shoulders back as if you are trying to touch your shoulder blades together. Hold for a count of 5. Relax for a count of 5.

Tense your shoulders by raising them toward your ears as if shrugging and holding for a count of 5. Relax for a count of 5.

Tighten your neck first by gently moving your head back (as if looking at the ceiling) and holding for 5. Relax for 5. Then gently drop your head forward and hold for 5. Relax for a count of 5.

Tighten your face muscles. First open your mouth wide and hold for 5. Relax for 5. Then raise your eye brows up high and hold for 5. Relax for 5. Finally clench your eyes tightly shut and hold for 5. Relax (with eyes gently closed) for 5.

Finish the exercise with breathing. Breathe in slowly through your nose, counting to 5. Hold the breath for a count of 5. Breathe out slowly, counting to five. Repeat 4 times. And that's it!

Perform this exercise whenever you need to relax, whether it's on a plane or in a car or anyplace else you may be sitting. Because this exercise may be very relaxing, it should not be performed while driving.

Over time, if performed regularly, this exercise will help you recognize tension in your body. You will be able to relax muscles at any time rather than performing the entire exercise. Perform at least twice a day for long-term results.

You may develop your own longer relaxation exercise by adding more muscle groups. Pinpoint your own areas of tension then tense and relax these areas in the same way.

Maximize the relaxation benefits of this exercise by visualizing a peaceful scene at the end of the exercise. Visualize a scene - a place where you feel relaxed - in detail for at least 5 minutes. Remember the happy place? Go there and enjoy it!

CONCLUSION

There is NO WAY to completely eliminate stress from your life. What you can do is to learn how to make that stress work FOR you.

Stress management isn't as difficult as it might actually seem. However, if you think you have too much stress in your life, it may be helpful to talk with your doctor, spiritual advisor, or local mental health association. Reactions to stress can be a factor in depression, anxiety and other disorders. They might suggest that you visit with a psychiatrist, psychologist, social worker, or other qualified counselor.

The author is not a medical professional. This book should be used as a tool that will help you cope with stress. Stress management tips are simple cost effective methods to effectively check stress. They can be practiced almost anywhere and at anytime.

Stress is a normal part of life and in small quantities it's good. It can motivate you and help you be more productive. However, too much stress, or a strong response to stress, is harmful.

It can set you up for general poor health as well as specific physical or psychological illnesses like infection, heart disease, or depression. Persistent and unrelenting stress often leads to anxiety and unhealthy behaviors like overeating and abuse of alcohol or drugs.

Just like causes of stress differ from person to person, what relieves stress is not the same for everyone. In general, however, making certain lifestyle changes as well as finding healthy, enjoyable ways to cope with stress helps most people.

Above all, remember that you are in no way alone in this battle. There are hundreds of thousands of people out there who feel overwhelmed too. Hopefully you will find peace within yourself and enjoy life to its fullest. When you feel yourself stressed out or beset with a panic attack, relax, breathe through it, and know that there are many, many people who feel exactly the same way.